YOUR KNOWLEDGE HAS VALUE

Stefanie Hoffmann

Are the 4 P's of international marketing of equal importance to all firms? What factors might cause some to more or less important than others?

A short article

GRIN Verlag

Bibliografische Information der Deutschen Nationalbibliothek:

Die Deutsche Bibliothek verzeichnet diese Publikation in der Deutschen National-
bibliografie; detaillierte bibliografische Daten sind im Internet über http://dnb.d-
nb.de/ abrufbar.

Imprint:

Copyright © 2005 GRIN Verlag GmbH
Druck und Bindung: Books on Demand GmbH, Norderstedt Germany
ISBN: 978-3-638-93007-9

This book at GRIN:

http://www.grin.com/en/e-book/55109/are-the-4-p-s-of-international-marketing-
of-equal-importance-to-all-firms

International Business Management

Are the 4 P´s of international marketing of equal importance to all firms? What factors might cause some to be more or less important than others?

by Stefanie Hoffmann

Nowadays marketing should be an indispensable part of all companies. Therefore many organisations and companies have marketing departments made up of marketing managers and specialists who have to coordinate the different areas of the marketing mix. Marketing has to be understood as a concept which stands at the beginning of the production process and which has to be integrated in all company areas. It describes the exact organisation, planning, execution and control of all company activities which should help to define customers´ wishes and expectations. (Lecture, Tourism Marketing, Bentele, Dr. B., Merkur Academy, 2004/2005) Nevertheless it is difficult to find an exact definition of marketing. Often it means different things to different people. As we are living in a fast-moving society, situations develop and change. The accepted UK definition is the one given by the Chartered Institute of Marketing: "Marketing is the management process which identifies, anticipates, and supplies customer requirements efficiently and profitably." (Lancaster and Massingham, 1999, p. 4)

In general, marketing is divided into strategic and operative marketing. In principle, the strategic marketing deals with the aims of the company, for example which competitors should be observed which markets are important or which target groups should be served with which products. The chosen strategies describe the way in which the company wants to reach their focused aims.

The operative marketing deals with the planning and execution of these strategies. With this aim in view, the company combines different marketing instruments which are known as the marketing mix. The most important marketing instruments are product, price, place and promotion, also known as the 4 P´s. This notion of the marketing mix is attributed to Neil H. Borden (1965) and refers to the set of marketing ingredients a company can use to achieve its objectives. (Lancaster and Massingham, 1995)

In order to answer the questions: "Are the 4 P´s of international marketing of equal importance to all firms? What factors might cause some to be more or less important than others?" the following explanations will be helpful.

The product is the basis or the foundation of the marketing mix because with no article there is nothing to promote, to price and to distribute. It means the totality of goods and services that the company offers to the target market and which are delivered to the consumer. "The actual product is that which gives satisfaction to the consumer, fulfilling the overall aim of marketing." (Lancaster and Reynolds, 1995, p. 93)
Without a product the marketing mix is a meaningless tool. All marketing planning is based on the product and must start from it. If the product is weak, it will not survive. Therefore companies must use new products as a mean towards market leadership, rather than market imitation. (Lancaster and Massingham, 1999) The aim of product policy is to offer a product or a service which has a Unique Selling Proposition (USP) in order to push out competitors.
Product policy is divided into product mix and product policy in the narrow sense. The product mix deals with number of the company's product lines (width) and the different kinds and variations within these special lines (length). One good example for describing this fact is the company Melitta. The range exists of things which deal with coffee (Melitta), for example coffee machines, coffee filter, coffee beans, all things which deal with tea (Cilia), cleanliness (Swirl), freezer bags (Toppits) and better living conditions (Aclimat).

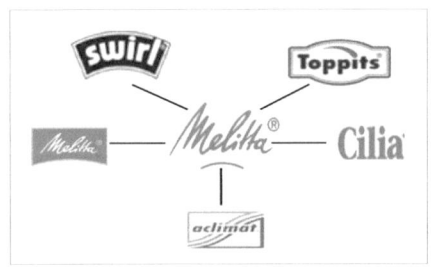

http://www.melitta.info/index.htm accessed on: 25.10.20

3

Typical decisions concerning product mix are product innovation or product changes. These depend on turnover, profit and the present market position. (Lecture, Tourism Marketing, Merkur Academy, Bentele, Dr.B., 2004/2005).

Product policy in the narrow sense deals with product design, brand policy, service policy and packaging. Product design covers the quality, style and supplementary functions of the individual product, brand policy decides whether a product should be offered as a no-name or proprietary article. Within the framework of packaging, design decisions concerning wrapping are made. Through the years it became more and more important because of the rising environmental consciousness of the consumer.
Especially the packaging of exclusive goods like watches is important because it reflects prestige and image.
The last point is service policy which includes special services like delivery franco domicile, extended guarantees or vouchers.

Price is a particularly potent element of the marketing mix because of its direct impact on the consumer, the company and the economy. To the consumer, price is a major indication of quality and an important factor in the decision-making process. "For the company, the price at which a product or service is sold represents the sole means of recouping costs and making a profit." (Lancaster and Reynolds, 1995, p. 46))
When introducing new products, the company has to develop pricing strategies. The two basic ones are the skimming and the penetration strategy.
The skimming strategy means that a company introduces a product at a high price to a small section of consumers (the early adopters). (Lancaster and Massingham, 1999) This strategy is recommendable for new technologies or innovations and if the product is unusually distinctive and demand is inelastic. The price will be lowered at successive stages when the product achieves larger sales.
The penetration strategy means that a product is introduced at a low price to attract the largest number of new buyers as soon as possible. The aim of the company is to gain a high market-share and to deter competitors.
In order to set a price the company has to inform itself about demand, costs, competitors and substitute products. After that, the company is able to choose the right strategy in order to determine the best price.

Another important fact concerning price is the condition policy. It includes credit conditions, for example leasing, discounts such as price reductions, and terms of payment and delivery.

Pricing decisions are said to be simple. If the company knows the costs of producing and marketing a product, it is easy to calculate the selling price and to change it if market conditions vary. (Lancaster and Massingham, 1999, p. 239) However, buyer and seller have different attitudes concerning the price of a product or service. For many people price is often an indicator of quality but if there are two equal products, consumers tend to buy the cheaper ones.

"Place includes company activities that make the product available to target consumers." (Kotler, Armstrong, Saunders, Wong, 1996, p. 96) The channel that a company uses to get its products to its customers is an important part of the marketing mix and can contribute to the customer's perception of the quality and value that the product provides. (CIM Companion, 2002)

Companies differentiate between direct distribution that means that they sell their goods directly to the final user, for example mail order catalogues or sales via internet and the selling through a series of intermediaries or middlemen, for example wholesaler or retailer who perform a variety of functions.

Producer →Consumer

Producer →Wholesaler →Customer

Producer →Wholesaler →Retailer →Consumer

(Lancaster and Massingham, 1999, p. 261)

The distribution chain has a number of advantages, for example costs of transport, storage and stock levels are reduced or the sheer number of transactions that must be made is dramatically reduced. (Lancaster and Reynolds, 1995)

Companies within the distribution chain depend on each other in order to meet the objectives and to satisfy customer needs. What kind of distribution channel a company should use depends on different factors. There are always advantages and disadvantages. Using the direct route to the customer, the company does not have to pay any commission for salesmen and it can ensure a high qualified consultation. The disadvantage is that the company needs enough capital in order to sell the goods all over the country. Using distribution channels the company has to pay commission and it does not have a direct contact to the customer. The advantage is that the companies have better expansion possibilities and that they have a high level of distribution. (Lecture, Tourism Marketing, Merkur Academy, Bentele, Dr. B., 2004/2005)

"Promotion is a means by which companies communicate the benefits of their products to their target markets." (Palmer and Hartley, 1996, p. 20)
It contains advertising, sales promotion, personal selling and public relations. As promotional methods need to be responsive to changes, direct marketing, sponsoring and product placement became also important.

Advertising is a non-personal form of mass communication that transmits its messages through various media. The most common forms are television, radio, newspapers or magazines.
Sales promotion involves the use of incentives to encourage customers to try and finally buy a product or service. This is often realised by using free gifts or samples, vouchers or discounts.
Personal selling deals with the direct contact to customers in order to make a sale and to build up a long-term relationship.
Public relations (PR) contain all measures used to demonstrate the goodwill of a company to achieve customer's confidence, for example press and annual reports. (Lecture, Tourism Marketing, Merkur Academy, Bentele, Dr. B., 2004/2005) All these communication instruments together are called promotional mix. Nearly all companies will have different promotional mixes which depend, for example on the product, consumer expectations, the size and of course the philosophy of the company. (Lancaster and Reynolds, 1995)

The aim of the communication policy can be described in the so called AIDA formula:

A	-	**Attention**
I	-	**Interest**
D	-	**Desire**
A	-	**Action**

(Lancaster and Massingham, 1999, p. 311)

The main idea is to draw the customers´ attention to the product in order to arouse their curiosity and to activate desire that they finally make a purchase with the aim to increase company sales.

The intention of every company has to be the improvement of the marketing mix. All instruments have to be carefully coordinated in order to reach the strategic aims. As there are different interactions between the instruments it is hardly realizable. Companies have to develop a sustainable competitive advantage over its competitors and they have to take into consideration that there are certain factors which influence the instruments of the marketing mix for example when doing business abroad. Having analysed the new market, all companies have to make marketing decisions in order to be able to enter the market successfully.

Regarding the product, some countries have different rules and regulations which have to be observed. In Germany for example it is not possible to drive an American car because of the different lighting. Another important point are the attitudes, habits and cultures of a foreign country. For McDonalds it is absolutely inconceivable to sell the regular product range in India / Bangladesh / Sri Lanka because cows are sacred. (Lecture, International Business Management, Breverton,T., UWIC, 2005) Therefore all companies have to adapt their products to local markets. Other factors which influence product decisions are the companies´ competitors. For example the low cost airline Ryanair which is strong in the UK and Ireland threatened German airlines because of establishing new bases and flying the same routes. Thus, careful research methods for example with the help of town's chamber of commerce or industry associations are advisable in order to identify companies´ competitors. (http://www.entrepreneur.com/article/0,4621,227044-2,00.html accessed on: 25.10.2005)
Every company has a main product. Car companies like Mercedes and BMW have their main focus on it. As customers know that the cars are of high quality and that they have a very good reputation they are prepared to pay a high price. Therefore it is possible for the company to neglect other marketing instruments like promotion or place.

Concerning price, companies have to charge different prices in different markets. They have to deal with different kinds of taxes, especially the rates of value added tax. The costs of producing, personnel costs or the costs of renting a store influence the price determination and therefore the weighting of this marketing instrument. Also regulations can limit price freedom.

Nowadays customers´ expectations are very different. As the markets are saturated and people have less money, they have to pay attention to the price.

Price wars between companies are the result of the present economic situation. The winners are for example low cost airlines like Ryanair. The firm immediately reacted to that in form of a rigorous low-price-policy and is now market leader in this business segment. It has early recognised that for the company the marketing instrument price is the most important one. In tourism product and place form one unity. Changes regarding the product will always lead to price changes. Therefore tourist organisations have their main focus on both marketing instruments, product and price.

The form of distribution often decides on success or failure of a product. McDonalds for example only reaches satisfying turnovers at highly frequented places like city centres or motorways. Designers like Gucci, Prada or Chanel also know that they must open their stores in areas where they can find the desired clientele (New York – Fifth Avenue, Paris - Champs Élysées…). Therefore a careful production site analysis is very essential. Companies like Amazon sell their goods only via internet whereas other ones only use direct distribution because of having contact to the customer. Consumers´ attitudes and the way they shop also influence companies´ distribution decisions and the level of weighting of the marketing instrument place.

Many companies have fast-selling-items in their product mixes. Therefore the marketing instrument promotion is less important, as consumers buy the goods anyway for example tissues like Kleenex (Kimberly-Clark). Other firms especially, newly founded ones have to spend a lot of money on marketing campaigns also when introducing new products. When preparing advertising campaigns all companies have to be careful especially when advertising abroad in order to avoid cultural clashes.

(Palmer and Hartley, 1996)

Choosing the right proportion of every single marketing instrument is always difficult. It always depends on the size of the company and especially on its budget. Another important point is the number of employees and their qualifications, finance, sales, production... (Maitland, 1998) If there are for example smaller companies they often have to hire advertising agencies for launching their marketing campaigns which leads to further payments. Therefore analysing the own company, the surrounding and the relevant sales market are indispensable elements when making marketing decisions.

Nevertheless there is a vast array of circumstances that will dictate which elements of the marketing mix have to be employed and in which proportion. If a company has put sufficient time into accurately analyses it becomes much easier to carry out this task. Of course, it takes time to think about marketing strategies and it will be difficult to make the right decisions. The most difficult ones are those where a company has to decide not to do certain things. The advantage of taking such decisions are, that it helps a company to focus on a more limited and achievable set of objectives. As a result it becomes clearer which elements of the marketing mix need to be used and therefore the company will be able to achieve profitable results.

Neil. H. Bordon said: "Like many concepts, the marketing mix concept seems relatively simple, once it has been expressed. Marketing and the building of marketing mixes will largely lie in the realm of art." (Bordon, 1984, pp.1-12)

Bibliography

Books

CIM Companion (2002) Marketing operations, Berkshire: CIM Publishing

Kottler, P., Armstrong, G., Saunders, J. and Wong, V. (1996) Principles of Marketing, Hertfordshire: Prentice Hall Europe

Lancaster, G. and Massingham, L. (1999) Essentials of Marketing, Berkshire: McGraw-Hill Publishing Company

Lancaster, G. and Reynolds, P. (1998) Marketing, Oxford: Butterworth-Heinemann

Maitland, I. (1998) The small business marketing handbook, London: Wellington House

Palmer, S. and Hartley, B. (1996) The business and marketing environment, Berkshire: McGraw-Hill Publishing Company

Journals

Bordon, Neil H. (1984) "The concept of the marketing mix", Journal of Advertising Research, Vol. 2, pp.7-12, September

Internet

http://www.melitta.info/index.htm accessed on: 25.10.2005

http://www.entrepreneur.com/article/0,4621,227044-2,00.html accessed on: 25.10.200

Lecture

Lecture, Tourism Marketing, Bentele, Dr. B., Merkur Academy, 2004/2005

Lecture, International Business Management, Breverton, T., UWIC, 2005